Reading

AGE 5-7

Rhona Whiteford and Jim Fitzsimmons
Illustrated by Lorna Kent

As a parent, you can play an important role in your child's education by your interest and encouragement. This book is designed to help your child become more confident in reading. There are four sections, each with a short test.

How to help your child

*   Keep sessions short and regular. A short period of work every day is usually more effective than a long session once a week

*   Build your child's confidence by offering lots of praise and encouragement. Rather than simply pointing out that an answer is wrong, you could say, 'You were almost right. Let's try again together!'

*   This book is not intended to teach your child to read from scratch, but builds on skills which will have been learned at school.

*   Encourage your child to see how reading can be both useful (finding out information, following instructions) and enjoyable (reading a story).

*   Don't treat the tests too formally. You can keep a running total of results on the chart on page 23. Encourage your child to sign the certificate when the book is completed. A sense of achievement is a great motivator!

Hodder
Children's
Books

The only home learning programme supported by the NCPTA

People

Complete these sentences using the words provided. The pictures below will give you a clue.

man	woman	boy	girl

This [_____] is a bus-driver.

This [_____] is painting a picture.

This [_____] is riding a bicycle.

This [_____] is a teacher.

This [_____] is playing a guitar.

This [_____] is cleaning the car.

Labels

Read the words in the box at the foot of the page, then write each word next to the right body part.

foot	shoulder	neck	hand
waist	elbow	ankle	leg
head	arm	knee	finger

Picture clues

Look at the picture, then read the questions. Answer them by underlining the correct word.

Who is throwing the ball? ▶ the girl/the boy

What is floating on the pond? ▶ box/boat

What is the boy flying? ▶ kite/kitten

How many people can you see? ▶ three/five

What is in the tree? ▶ ball/nest

Is the sun shining? ▶ yes/no

What is looking over the fence? ▶ house/horse

Look at the picture, then try to make a complete sentence by matching the beginnings with the endings. Draw lines to join them up.

One boy is	by the gate.
Two children are	on the slide.
The park-keeper is	feeding the ducks.
One girl is	on the roundabout.
Three people are	cutting the hedge.
One person is	on the swing.
There is a castle	lying down reading.
The gardener is	in the sandpit.

Instructions

Read these sentences to see how to colour this clown.

Colour his hair orange.

Colour his shirt blue.

Colour his nose red.

Colour the patch on his trousers yellow.

Colour the dots on his bowtie red.

Give him pink braces.

Colour the flowers yellow and blue.

Give him striped trousers.

Now you can use any other colours to finish off your clown.

Signs

Look at the picture and work out what is going on. Then read the signs below. Can you number the signs so they match the numbered places in the picture correctly?

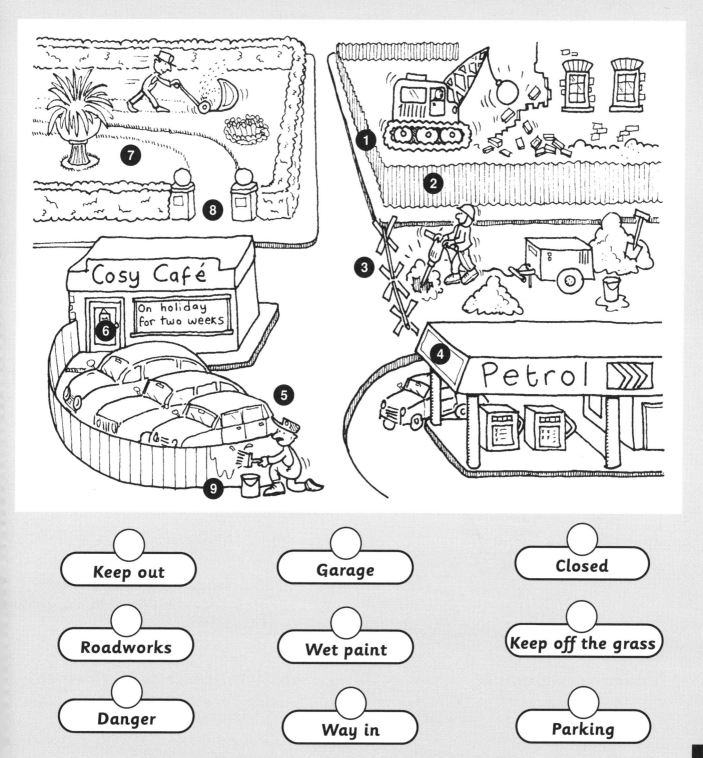

Keep out

Garage

Closed

Roadworks

Wet paint

Keep off the grass

Danger

Way in

Parking

■ TEST I ■

Try to read the story in full. Score one point for each word guessed correctly.

This is a little called Peter. He was going on holiday on an

 . First he had to pack his . He put in a

pair of and his best and a pair of . He

also put in a pair of and a large  . Now he was

ready. He got his passport and and went to the

 . Soon the aeroplane was high in the

 . After a smooth flight they

landed safely and a  was waiting to take them to

8

the  .

The was shining and the was bumpy but soon

he was sunbathing by the 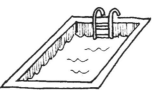 . He ate a huge

 as he read his favourite . The in

the hotel was delicious and Peter had a wonderful holiday. The

 weeks passed quickly and Peter was very when

the came to return home.

Match the rhyming words. Draw lines to join them together.

sing	mouse	gain	best
clock	flower	through	thank
house	tramp	time	stain
cramp	ring	blank	climb
shower	block	nest	blue

You can complete the sentences below by writing in words from the box beneath.

Mary and Peter had a day trip.

They went to the _____ .

The tickets cost _____ _____ .

They saw lots of _____ .

Their favourite animal was the _____ .

They bought an ____ - _____ .

They went home on the ____ .

animals   elephant   zoo   bus   two pounds   ice-cream

Arrange the words below to make proper sentences so that you can read the story.

| wicked make very to Aladdin rich. uncle A promised |

▶

| had a get lamp an He from to cave. underground magic |

▶

| genie marry princess. the to helped The Aladdin |

▶

| end wicked the was In the defeated. uncle |

▶

| his and happily lived ever princess Aladdin after. |

▶

Complete this story by writing in words from the box beneath.

One morning Kate found a large _____ at the bottom of the

_____ . She took it _____ , and put it on the

_____ . The egg cracked and out popped a baby _____ .

He was _____ and could grant _____ . Kate wished

for a _____ and a _____ _____ .

garden	radiator	egg	dragon	inside	wishes
computer	game	magic	bicycle		

Magic **e** changes the sound of each of these letters to the sound shown below it.

a	e	i	o	u
[ay]	[ee]	[eye]	[oh]	[you]

Make new words by adding an **e** to the letters below. Say each word out loud.

gat __   ston __   cub __

tub __   mic __   ros __

lan __   bon __   cut __

thes __   smil __   rid __

hos __   rak __   pal __

■ TEST 2 ■

Look at the picture, then, as quickly as you can, underline the word in the same row that goes with it. Score one point for each correct word. Allow yourself a maximum of two minutes.

| rose | hotel | rocket | shop | pocket | stamp |

| flame | tree | money | frog | flag | gun |

| cat | cap | orange | ball | car | gun |

| leaf | fig | nest | fish | dog | flash |

| jug | land | ladder | lamp | clock | clamp |

| door | bee | roof | dog | goat | food |

| shoe | kite | bow | shine | ship | shot |

| doll | ball | dog | nail | bull | bell |

| hose | house | mouse | horse | heat | head |

| ship | shy | shop | stone | shoe | star |

Reading carefully

Read these sentences carefully, then write **true** or **false** next to them.

A man has walked on Mars. ▶

Spaghetti is a type of pasta. ▶

All snakes are poisonous. ▶

A daffodil is a yellow flower. ▶

Cavemen had electric fires. ▶

An eagle is a bird of prey. ▶

Read the instructions carefully.

Yachts with two sails can travel fast. Colour the slow yachts blue.

Cats which have been fed go to sleep. Colour the hungry cats brown.

Birds that can sing sit on the branches. Colour the birds that can't sing yellow.

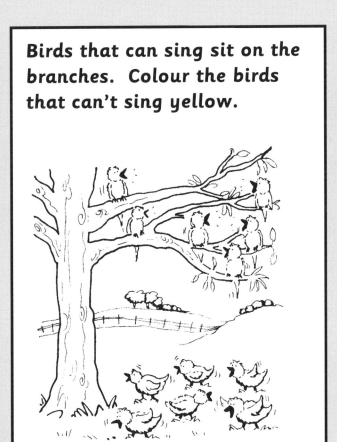

The bins with a number on are full. Colour the empty bins green.

Put these sentences in the right order by numbering them from 1 to 6.

She threw a ball for Sam.

It bounced into a deep hole.

Helen's big brother pulled Sam out.

Helen took her dog Sam for a walk.

Sam went down the hole and got stuck.

Sam chased after the ball.

Speak like me

Match the words to the right person, then read them in the sort of voice that you think they might have.

Fee, fi, fo, fum,
I smell the blood of an Englishman.
Be he alive or be he dead,
I'll grind his bones to make my bread.

Whoooo! Whoooo! Whoooo!
I am the ghost of old Sir Ned,
I upset the king and lost my head.

Hubble-bubble, toil and trouble,
See the witches' cauldron bubble.
Swirling colours, awful smell,
All to make a magic spell.

I am programmed to do exactly as you wish. Key in my instructions for today.

Avast and belay there me hearties. Let's hoist the rigging and set sail for Treasure Island.

Daddy, Daddy, I want my teddy bear, and I want a drink of water.

■ TEST 3 ■

Read the description very carefully, then using the description draw and colour a picture, including as many details as you can. You will need a separate sheet of paper for your drawing.

1 The king was very tall and thin with long black hair and a drooping moustache.

2 On his head he wore a golden crown.

3 He had a cruel face and he looked angry.

4 He was wearing a long tunic which almost reached the floor.

5 This was dark blue with a golden dragon design on it.

6 On his arms and legs you could see grey chain-mail.

7 In his left hand he held a great golden sword.

8 Resting at his feet was a large oval shield.

9 This was also dark blue with the same golden dragon design on it.

10 He stood by the gate of the castle as if ready to defend it against anyone.

Score one point for including all the details from each sentence.

SCORE
/10

17

Finding out

Look at the volumes of an encyclopedia shown below. On the spine of each book there are letters of the alphabet and a number. Each volume contains information about subjects which begin with the letters of the alphabet on its spine.

Look at the topics below and decide which volume of the encyclopedia might contain information about it. Put the number in the box.

cars **2**   America ⬜   wildlife ⬜   zoos ⬜

kings and queens ⬜   ships ⬜   space travel ⬜

music ⬜   trees ⬜   flying ⬜   buildings ⬜

stamps ⬜   machines ⬜   art ⬜   India ⬜

composers ⬜   inventions ⬜   dinosaurs ⬜

plants ⬜   sport ⬜   scientists ⬜

China ⬜   birds ⬜   Eskimos ⬜

Choose the right book

Write the title of the book where you might expect to find the answers to these questions.

Who designed St Paul's Cathedral in London? ▶

Who was Julius Caesar? ▶

When is the best time to plant daffodils? ▶

Where does coral grow? ▶

Where were the 1992 Olympic Games held? ▶

Why does an owl sleep during the day? ▶

What is the 'Space Shuttle'? ▶

Who was Queen of England in 1850? ▶

How do you make an omelette? ▶

What is tyrannosaurus rex? ▶

Scanning

Glance very quickly at the picture below, then write down the answers to the questions.

To make this harder, cover the picture before attempting the questions.

How many animals can you see? ▶

Can you see three vehicles? ▶

How many giraffes can you see? ▶

What is in the tree? ▶

How many birds can you see? ▶

How many people are there? ▶

What is the lion doing? ▶

What is in the grass? ▶

Predicting

Read the passage, then try to decide what happens next. Turn the page upside down to see if our ending is the same as yours.

John and Sally crawled through the open cellar window into the inky blackness within. At first they could see nothing as they fumbled in the darkness looking for a place to hide. They crawled underneath a large table. They would be safe there. Suddenly, piercing the silence, the door of the cellar burst open. John and Sally could clearly see the outline of a large figure with outstretched arms coming towards them. It seemed to know exactly where to look. It came closer and reached under the table. Sally closed her eyes and screamed.

'Gotcha!' Two strong arms lifted Sally from under the table.
'Oh, Dad, how did you know where to find us?' asked John.
'You always come here when we play hide-and-seek. Now, one more game before it's time for bed,' replied their father.

■ TEST 4 ■

Read the following passage, then answer the questions. Score one point for each correct answer.

> Summer begins in June and ends in September. It is usually warm and sunny in summer. The flowers in the gardens are really beautiful and the trees are covered in leaves. The summer sun ripens the farmer's crops in the fields and greenhouses, ready for the harvest. Sometimes, if it gets too hot and too dry, we may be short of water. Most people take a holiday in summer and they wear shorts and T-shirts to keep cool.

When does summer begin? ▶

What are the trees covered in? ▶

What does the summer sun do? ▶

What can happen if it gets too hot and dry? ▶

When do most people take a holiday? ▶

What do people wear to keep cool? ▶

What are the flowers like in summer? ▶

When does summer end? ▶

SCORE

/8

22

RECORD OF SUCCESS

TEST 1	TEST 2	TEST 3	TEST 4	TOTAL
22	10	10	8	50

Well done! Now tick one of these boxes.

I am very pleased   quite pleased   not at all pleased with myself.

✳ ✳ ✳ ✳ ✳ ✳ ✳ CERTIFICATE ✳ ✳ ✳ ✳ ✳ ✳ ✳

This is to certify that

_____

has successfully completed the work in this book on reading and has done very well.

signed _____

date _____

Answers

Test 1

boy, aeroplane, suitcase, shorts, teeshirt, swimming trunks, sunglasses, hat, ticket, airport, clouds, coach, hotel, sun, road, swimming pool, ice-cream, book, food, two, sad, time.   Total 22

Test 2

rocket, flag, car, fish, ladder, door, ship, bell, house, shoe.   Total 10

Test 3

Award one point when all the details given in a sentence appear in the drawing.   Total 10

Test 4

June, leaves, ripens crops, water shortage, summer, shorts and teeshirts, really beautiful, September. Total 8

Total points for tests: 50

Copyright ©Rhona Whiteford and Jim Fitzsimmons 1994

The right of Rhona Whiteford and Jim Fitzsimmons to be identified as the authors of the Work has been asserted by them in accordance with the Copyright, Designs and Patents Act 1988.

Published by Hodder Children's Books 1995   ISBN 0 340 65107 5   10 9 8 7 6 5 4 3 2 1

Printed and bound in Great Britain

Hodder Children's Books
A division of Hodder Headline plc
338 Euston Road
London NW1 3BH

Previously published as Headstart Basics: Reading